KNOW IT
ANCIENT EGYPT

By Louise Nelson

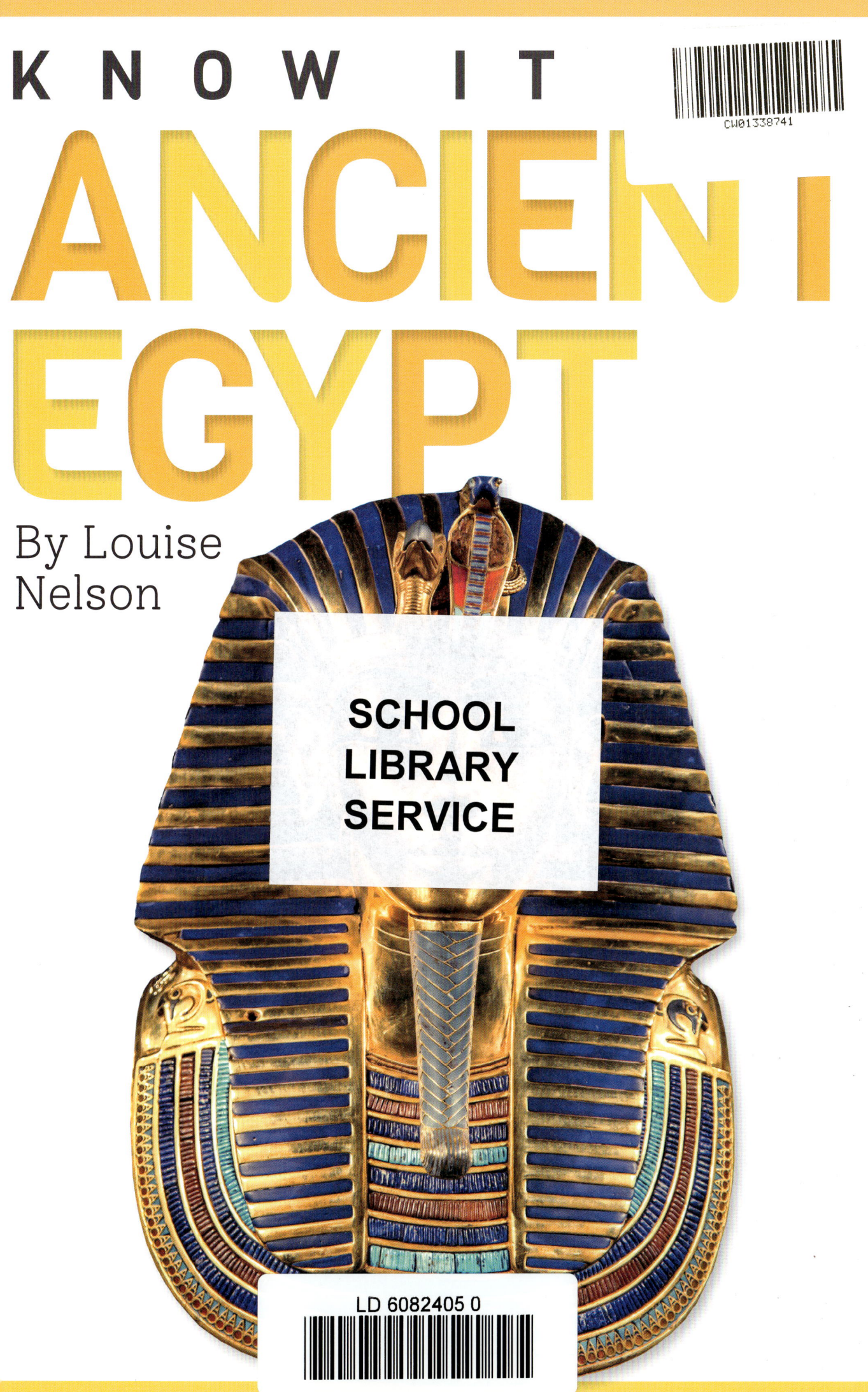

BookLife
PUBLISHING

©2022
BookLife Publishing Ltd.
King's Lynn, Norfolk
PE30 4LS, UK

All rights reserved.
Printed in Poland.

A catalogue record for this book is available from the British Library.

ISBN: 978-1-80155-673-6

Written by:
Louise Nelson

Edited by:
William Anthony

Designed by:
Dan Scase

All facts, statistics, web addresses and URLs in this book were verified as valid and accurate at time of writing. No responsibility for any changes to external websites or references can be accepted by either the author or publisher.

PHOTO CREDITS

All images are courtesy of Shutterstock.com. With thanks to Getty Images, Thinkstock Photo and iStockphoto.
Front cover: bogdan ionescu, Paul Fleet, Taigi, viritphon, Dario Lo Presti, Kamira, Daria Volyanskaya, YuRi Photolife, QBR, Anan Kaewkhammul, Photo Win1, Jaroslav Moravcik, Cholpan, Marti Bug Catcher. 4&5 – BORTEL Pavel – Pavelmidi, totophotos, Dmytro Buianskyi, Lars Poyansky, Ewa Studio, agsaz, Prachaya Roekdeethaweesab, Scott Rothstein, Musicheart7, bogdan ionescu, Marti Bug Catcher, In Green, Noel V. Baebler, DIRECTMEDIA. 6&7 – Catmando, takepicsforfun, grintan, Jaroslav Moravcik, Vladimir Wrangel. 8&9 – Peter Hermes Furian, Tanya_mtv, Grigorev Mikhail, Andrei Dubadzel, S-F, Krasovski Dmitri. 10&11 – Eric Gaba, Rashevskyi Viacheslav, Met Museum, Macquarie University, Marti Bug Catcher, airphoto.gr, Gorbash Varvara. 12&13 – tan_tan, Claudia Paulussen. 14&15 – tan_tan, marina.soboleva, Maciek67, hemro. 16&17 – OlgaChernyak, Ivan Soto Cobos, Dario Lo Presti, Andrea Izzotti, Scott Rothstein, Rama, Wellcome Images, Federico Rostagno. 18&19 – Jaroslav Moravcik, Ivan Soto Cobos, Squeeb Creative, Jakub Kyncl, Guenter Albers. 20&21 – Aleksandr Pobedimskiy, Petr Bonek, Merydolla. 22&23 – Ingotr, Eroshka. 24&25 – Keith Wheatley, Nerthuz, Hayati Kayhan, matrioshka, Metropolitan Museum of Art. 26&27 – Abrilla, Walters Art Museum, FwFegn4zfljkZA at Google Cultural Institute, MM_photos. 28&29 – Michelle Lee Photography, MAX2MAX, Soifi, bigacis, Lotus Images, Maks Narodenko, Kovaleva_Ka, Ingotr, photomaster, matrioshka. 30&31 – agsaz, Jaroslav Moravcik, Hayati Kayhan, Marti Bug Catcher, Kamira, Andrey Burmakin, Ivan Soto Cobos, Ingotr, Eroshka, Nikolai Tsvetkov. 32&33 – Jaroslav Moravcik, leksandar Mijatovic, Beatrice Barberis, pegasusa012, Marti Bug Catcher, Roman Silantev. 34&35 – Tim UR, Serg64, Maderla, doomu, Daemys, Valentina Razumova, pickingpok. 36&37 – tan_tan, akimov konstantin, Noel V. Baebler, givaga, monicaodo, Mara Fribus.
Did you know vector: Liudmila Klymenko.

CONTENTS

Page 4	**Ancient Egypt**
Page 6	**Key Ideas**
Page 8	**Who Were the Ancient Egyptians?**
Page 10	**Timeline: Egypt**
Page 12	**Gods and Worship**
Page 14	**Pharaohs**
Page 16	**Death**
Page 18	**Pyramids**
Page 20	**Case Study: The Great Sphinx**
Page 22	**Daily Life**
Page 24	**Inventions**
Page 26	**Hieroglyphs**
Page 28	**Food**
Page 30	**The Ancient Egyptians**
Page 32	**Believe It or Not!**
Page 34	**Activity**
Page 36	**Quick Quizzes**
Page 38	**Glossary**
Page 40	**Index**

Words that look like this can be found in the glossary on page 38.
Key ideas you will need can be found on page 6.

ANCIENT EGYPT

Perhaps you've seen pictures of the pyramids, or dressed as a mummy for a fancy dress party? Everyone's heard of the ancient Egyptians – and it's not that surprising. This mighty civilisation lasted over 3,000 years, after all!

So, what do you think of when you think of ancient Egypt?

There is more to ancient Egypt than mummies and **tombs**. The ancient Egyptians were fascinating people and they did amazing things that we still study today. Why? Well, the ancient Egyptians left a lot of things behind. Now, we can see exactly how they lived, worshipped and even what they thought happened when they died.

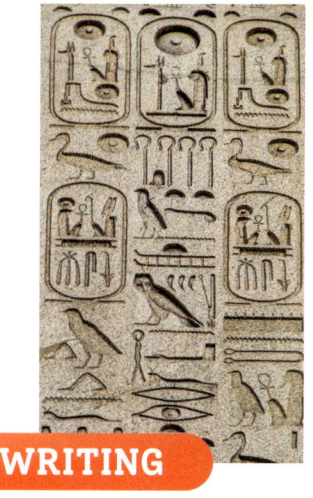

WRITING

THEMSELVES

BUILDINGS

LANGUAGE

ART

DID YOU KNOW?

The ancient Egyptians were thought to have invented many things that we use today, including toothbrushes, eye makeup and the plough!

PLOUGH

Pictures left by the ancient Egyptians show us how they lived, such as this picture of an Egyptian using a simple plough.

5

KEY IDEAS

CIVILISATION

A civilisation is a large group of people who all share an advanced way of living and working. A civilisation has some sort of government, which makes the rules people live by, and shared ways of living and working. Civilisations usually build up around cities and include the knowledge, fashions and religious beliefs of that group of people.

This is how an ancient Egyptian city might have looked. Egyptian civilisation grew around cities.

RELIGION

Many people believe in a **deity**, such as a god or goddess, many gods, or a higher power of some kind that can affect people here on Earth, and after they die. There are lots of different beliefs. Religions are a way to organise these beliefs and pass them on. Religions, such as Christianity, Islam and Hinduism, help people follow the same beliefs and **rituals** of worship, and usually have important people who are in charge.

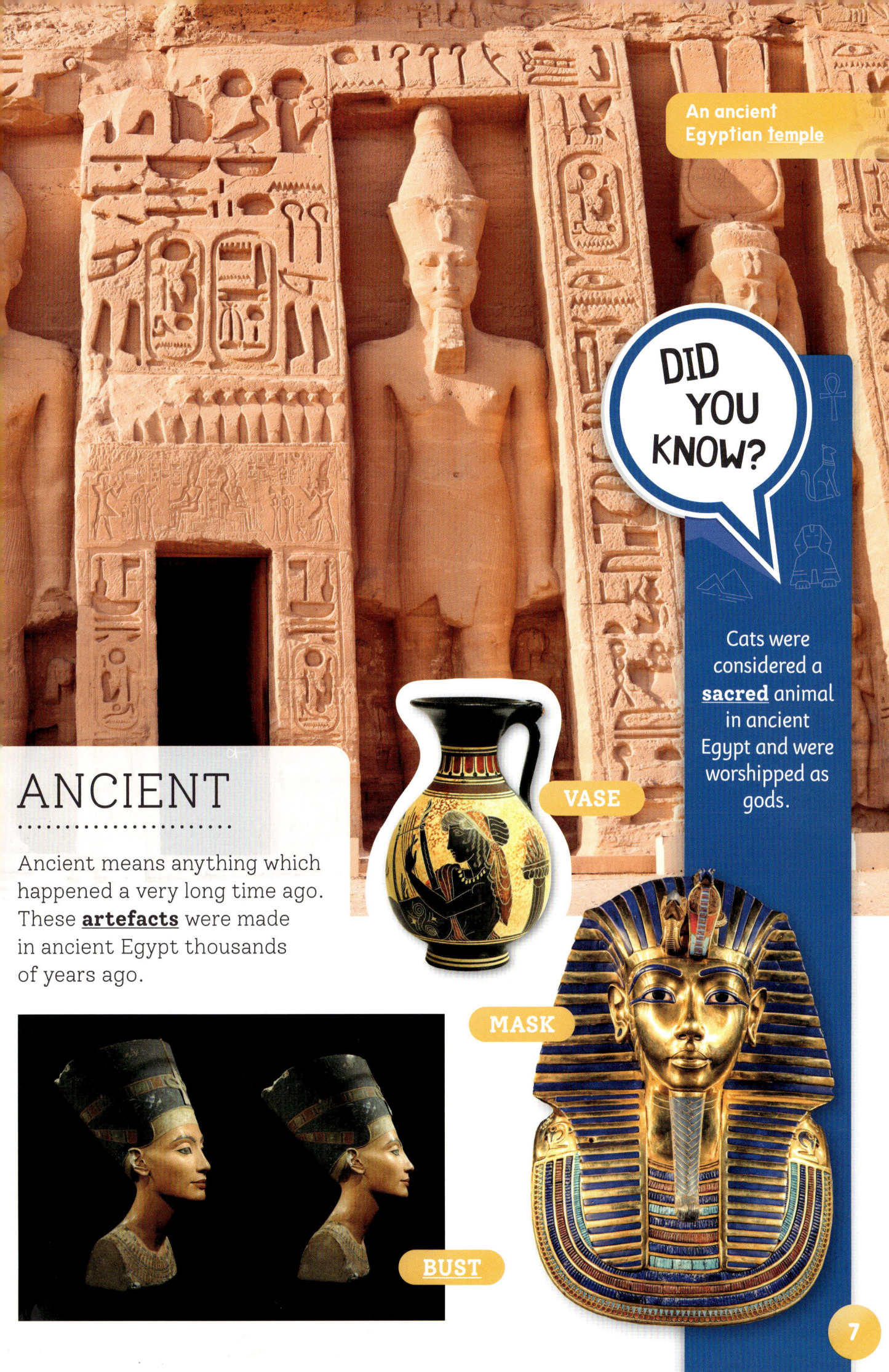

An ancient Egyptian temple

DID YOU KNOW?

Cats were considered a sacred animal in ancient Egypt and were worshipped as gods.

VASE

MASK

ANCIENT

Ancient means anything which happened a very long time ago. These **artefacts** were made in ancient Egypt thousands of years ago.

BUST

WHO WERE THE ANCIENT EGYPTIANS?

Around 5,000 years ago, people in northern Africa began building villages around the banks of the River Nile. Most of this area of Africa was sandy desert, where it was very hard to grow any food. Around the river, however, the soil was perfect for growing **crops**.

Wheat was an important crop for the ancient Egyptians.

Soil found around the banks of the Nile was perfect for growing crops.

Perch, like this one, can be caught in the River Nile.

The people living around the Nile lived well and were successful, so the Egyptian civilisation grew and grew! The river also provided the people with water, fish and a means of **transport**. They could use the mud and reeds to build houses and other things they needed.

Flax plants can be woven into clothing.

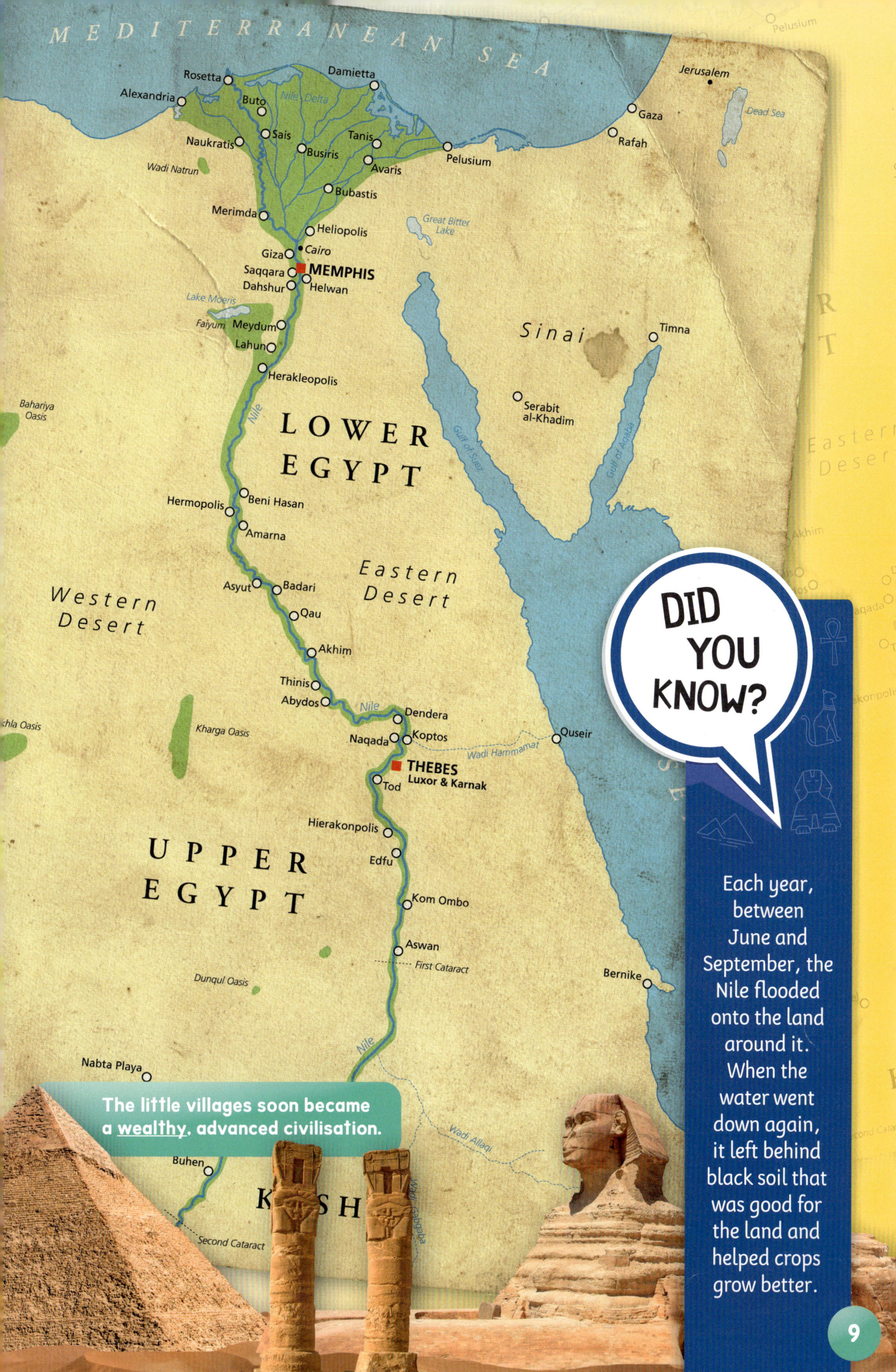

DID YOU KNOW?

Each year, between June and September, the Nile flooded onto the land around it. When the water went down again, it left behind black soil that was good for the land and helped crops grow better.

The little villages soon became a <u>wealthy</u>, advanced civilisation.

TIMELINE: EGYPT

2925 BC
THE EARLY DYNASTIC PERIOD

The first pharaoh of Egypt, Menes, unites Upper and Lower Egypt into a single civilisation ruled by one pharaoh. Memphis is the capital city of Egypt.

2575 BC
THE OLD KINGDOM
The Great Pyramids and the Great Sphinx were built.

1075 BC
THIRD INTERMEDIATE PERIOD
Egypt is divided again. It is invaded and ruled for a time by the Assyrian Empire.

1539 BC
THE NEW KINGDOM

This was a golden age of ancient Egypt. The civilisation enjoyed wealth and power.

664 BC
THE LATE PERIOD

ALEXANDER THE GREAT

Many different rulers struggle for power. Alexander the Great <u>conquers</u> Egypt for the Greeks.

332 BC
THE PTOLEMAIC DYNASTY
Ptolemy I, a Greek, is installed as pharaoh. Cleopatra VII, the last pharaoh, dies and Egypt is taken over by Rome.

2130 BC

THE FIRST INTERMEDIATE PERIOD

Egypt splits apart again and there are struggles for power.

MENTUHOTEP II

1938 BC

THE MIDDLE KINGDOM

Egypt is brought together again, united by Mentuhotep II.

ABISHA THE HYKSOS

1630 BC

THE SECOND INTERMEDIATE PERIOD

For a time, northern Egypt is taken over by the Hyksos dynasty, from Palestine.

30 BC

Rome takes over.

DID YOU KNOW?

BC stands for Before Christ. If you see this next to a date, it means this happened before the birth of Jesus Christ. When you see BC, you are counting backwards on the timeline.

GODS AND WORSHIP

The ancient Egyptians believed in many gods and goddesses. Some had certain things they were thought to look after, such as the **afterlife**, or the **harvest** of the crops. Many of the gods were thought to look like animals, such as jackals, birds and cats.

Khnum was the god of water.

Hathor was the goddess of women and the sky.

Sobek was the god of the Nile and was thought to have created the world.

12

Anubis was the god of mummies and the afterlife.

Sekhmet was a warrior goddess. She had the head of a lion. She was also the goddess of medicine.

Horus was the god of the Sun and sky, and watched over the pharaoh. Horus was thought to be a ruler of the gods, and was a very important god all across Egypt.

Isis was one of the oldest goddesses. She was thought to look after the dead, heal people and be a role model for women. She was worshipped all over Egypt and across the world.

People did things to keep the gods happy. They lived good lives and made offerings of gifts and animals. People worshipped these gods in temples.

13

PHARAOHS

The kings and queens of Egypt were called pharaohs. They were the most important people in the kingdom. The ancient Egyptians thought the pharaoh was like a living god. Most pharaohs were men, but some were women. Pharaohs would pass on the job to their children when they died. This is called a dynasty.

GREAT ROYAL WIFE

SERVANTS

PHARAOH

SLAVES

Pharaohs could have many wives, but the pharaoh's main wife was the most important. She was called the Great Royal Wife and was very powerful.

14

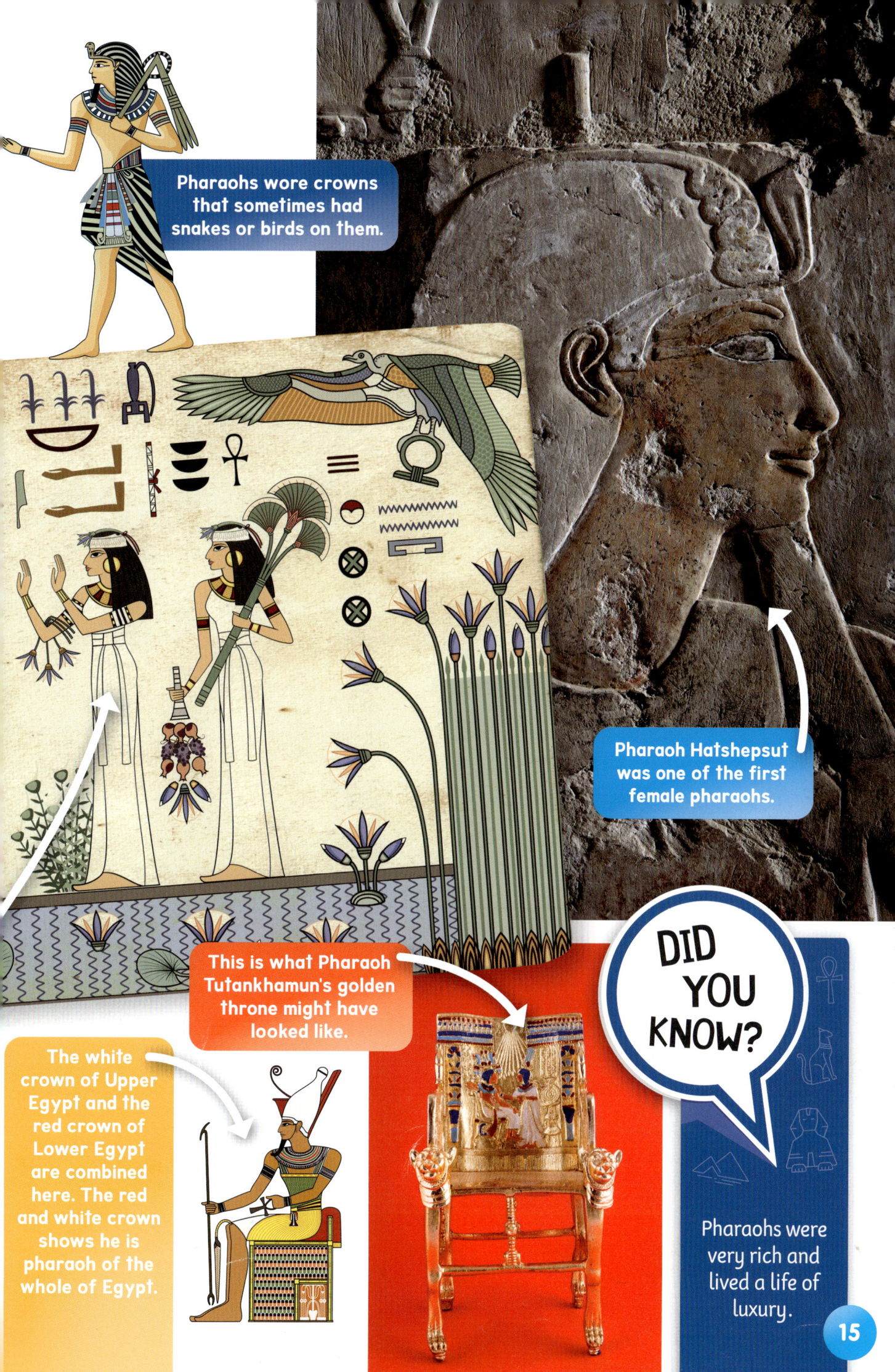

Pharaohs wore crowns that sometimes had snakes or birds on them.

Pharaoh Hatshepsut was one of the first female pharaohs.

This is what Pharaoh Tutankhamun's golden throne might have looked like.

The white crown of Upper Egypt and the red crown of Lower Egypt are combined here. The red and white crown shows he is pharaoh of the whole of Egypt.

DID YOU KNOW?

Pharaohs were very rich and lived a life of luxury.

DEATH

THE AFTERLIFE

The ancient Egyptians believed that, after you died, you had to face the tests of the gods to prove you had lived a good life on Earth. If you had, and you passed the tests, you could pass on into the afterlife and live in the Field of Reeds. There, life is just like on Earth, but there is no struggle and no death. Your loved ones would eventually join you there.

The dead person's heart is weighed by Anubis, and the weight is compared to the feather of truth. If the heart is heavier, it must be full of bad deeds, and the heart is eaten by Ammit, a god with body parts of a crocodile, a lion and a hippopotamus. The person cannot then pass to the afterlife.

MUMMIFICATION

Once a good soul had entered the Field of Reeds, the body still had to go somewhere. The body had its **internal organs** removed, except the heart. Then, it was filled with sweet spices and **preserved**. The body was finally wrapped in linen. This process is called mummification.

Mummies were placed in a coffin. If the person was very important or wealthy, the coffin might be put inside a sarcophagus, such as this one.

Cats were often mummified too!

The internal organs were placed in special jars, called canopic jars.

This is a mummified head.

Tools like this were used to remove the brain and organs.

You can see mummies in museums today.

The body had to be preserved so the soul could enter the Field of Reeds.

DID YOU KNOW?

The ancient Egyptians didn't have a word that meant death – at least, in terms of not being alive anymore. They thought death was just another stage on the journey of life.

PYRAMIDS

Tomb walls were painted with stories and information for the person in the afterlife. to help them know what was happening and what to do.

After mummification, poorer Egyptians would be buried in the sand. Pharaohs got special treatment. The mummies of the pharaohs were laid to rest inside huge pyramids. This happened mostly in the Old Kingdom and Middle Kingdom. Pharaohs were buried with treasures, animals, chariots and sometimes even slaves to help them in the afterlife.

CHARIOT

TREASURES FOR THE AFTERLIFE

BURIAL MASK

DID YOU KNOW?

The base of a pyramid is always perfectly square.

18

Around 50 royal pyramids still stand. The most famous are the Great Pyramids of Giza, shown here. The largest is made from over 2 million blocks of rock.

DID YOU KNOW?

Even to this day, no one knows for sure how the pyramids were built.

CASE STUDY: THE GREAT SPHINX

LIMESTONE

Near the Great Pyramids stands a massive **sculpture** looking over the sands. At 20 metres tall and 73 metres long, this massive figure is made of limestone, with a lion's body and a man's head. This is the Great Sphinx, one of the world's largest sculptures.

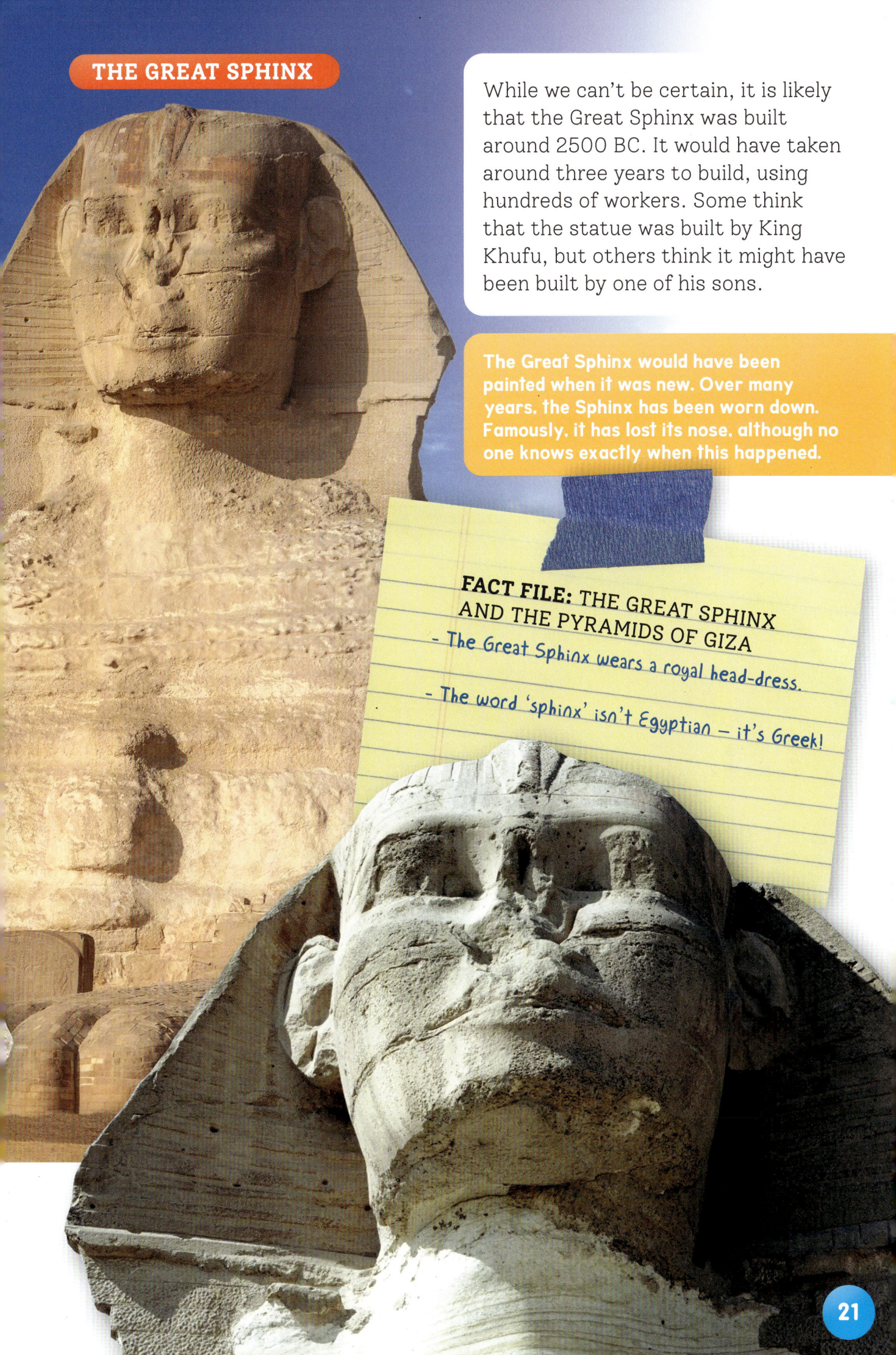

THE GREAT SPHINX

While we can't be certain, it is likely that the Great Sphinx was built around 2500 BC. It would have taken around three years to build, using hundreds of workers. Some think that the statue was built by King Khufu, but others think it might have been built by one of his sons.

The Great Sphinx would have been painted when it was new. Over many years, the Sphinx has been worn down. Famously, it has lost its nose, although no one knows exactly when this happened.

FACT FILE: THE GREAT SPHINX AND THE PYRAMIDS OF GIZA

- The Great Sphinx wears a royal head-dress.
- The word 'sphinx' isn't Egyptian – it's Greek!

DAILY LIFE

In ancient Egypt, there was a clear **social order**. The people at the top were the most important. The gods and the pharaoh were at the very top. People in the government came next, then scribes. **Peasants** were near the bottom, and at the very bottom were the slaves.

- GODS
- PHARAOH
- VIZIER, SENIOR OFFICIALS, HIGH PRIESTS AND NOBLES
- SCRIBES
- SKILLED ARTISANS AND CRAFTSPEOPLE
- PEASANT FARMERS AND WORKERS
- SERVANTS AND SLAVES

Scribes were people who could read and write. Being a scribe was an honour in ancient Egypt.

FARMER

The ancient Egyptians had families, jobs and homes, just like we do today. Many families had children, and children usually learned to do the same job as their parents. Most people wore loose clothes to keep cool, and lived in houses made of mud, baked hard by the hot Sun. Here are some common jobs that people in ancient Egypt might have had.

HUNTER

PRIEST

Artisans made pottery and other crafts.

DID YOU KNOW?

Both men and women could have important jobs in ancient Egypt. Women could be priestesses, supervisors and even pharaoh.

INVENTIONS

The ancient Egyptians invented lots of things to help them live better lives. Let's take a look at some ancient Egyptian inventions.

The ancient Egyptians were the first people that we know of to use makeup and wigs. Lots of Egyptian makeup was made from <u>toxic</u> things.

The ancient Egyptians were the first people to have an actual police force, with people specially trained to keep the peace.

Papyrus was a type of paper made from reeds. The ancient Egyptians wrote on it with ink, made from ground-up <u>materials</u> mixed with water.

The ancient Egyptians invented brushing teeth. Toothpaste was made by grinding up salt with flowers, ashes and eggshells. This paste could be rubbed on with a finger, or with a toothbrush made from a stick with a frayed end.

Before the ancient Egyptians, people used stools, but the Egyptians invented tables and chairs with backs.

25

HIEROGLYPHS

Hieroglyphs carved into a wall

The ancient Egyptians used a type of writing called hieroglyphs. Hieroglyph means 'sacred carving', because the ancient Egyptians believed that writing had been invented by the gods. Hieroglyphs are pictures, and each picture has a different meaning. Scribes learned each of the hieroglyphs and could write them on papyrus or carve them into stone.

Some of the symbols in hieroglyphs mean whole words. These are called ideograms. Others mean sounds. These are called phonograms. So, a hieroglyph of an owl could mean 'owl', but it could also mean 'mmm'.

Important names were written inside an oval shape called a cartouche. This represented a rope to keep evil spirits away.

DID YOU KNOW?

Hieroglyphs could be written in either rows or columns. Look at the way the animals are facing. They always face the start of the writing. If they face left, the sentence goes from left to right. Columns are read top to bottom.

Can you write your name using these hieroglyphs? Don't forget to circle it in a cartouche!

27

FOOD

The ancient Egyptians ate a simple but healthy diet. They mostly ate fruit, vegetables, meat and bread. Meat, **dairy** and fish were more expensive, and poorer people were thought to have lived mostly on vegetables.

Because the Egyptians lived around the banks of the Nile, they could grow and harvest many crops, many of which we still eat today.

Emmer was the main grain grown in ancient Egypt.

Ancient Egyptian bread was very tough, and caused some people to have problems with their teeth.

The ancient Egyptians loved garlic – no wonder they invented the breath mint too!

CHICKPEAS

28

CUCUMBER

DATES AND DRIED FRUITS

Honey was an expensive treat.

Hunters would catch deer, goats and other animals.

Ducks and <u>poultry</u> sometimes provided meat for poorer families, who also ate mice and hedgehogs!

What Egyptian foods can you see in this painting?

THE ANCIENT EGYPTIANS

The ancient Egyptian civilisation lasted for almost 3,000 years and saw many changes along the way. From the pyramids at the beginning of their history up until they were taken over by ancient Rome, they were one of the most successful civilisations of ancient times.

THEY WERE:

- RULED BY GODS
- KINGS, QUEENS AND PHARAOHS
- INVENTORS AND SCIENTISTS
- BUILDERS AND ENGINEERS
- WRITERS AND HISTORIANS

MUMMIES

PRIESTS AND WORSHIPPERS

FARMERS

In fact, the people of ancient Egypt weren't that different from you and me!

CAT LOVERS

ARTISTS

DID YOU KNOW?

The ancient Egyptians left so many things behind that people spend their whole lives finding out about them. These people are called Egyptologists.

BELIEVE IT OR NOT!

Let's take a look at some fascinating facts about ancient Egypt.

BURIAL MASK

Tutankhamun was a young pharaoh. He died before he was even 20 years old.

Pharaohs did not pass into the Field of Reeds when they died. Instead, the ancient Egyptians believed that the pharaoh would be reborn as a god.

THOTH, THE GOD OF MAGIC, WRITING AND THE MOON

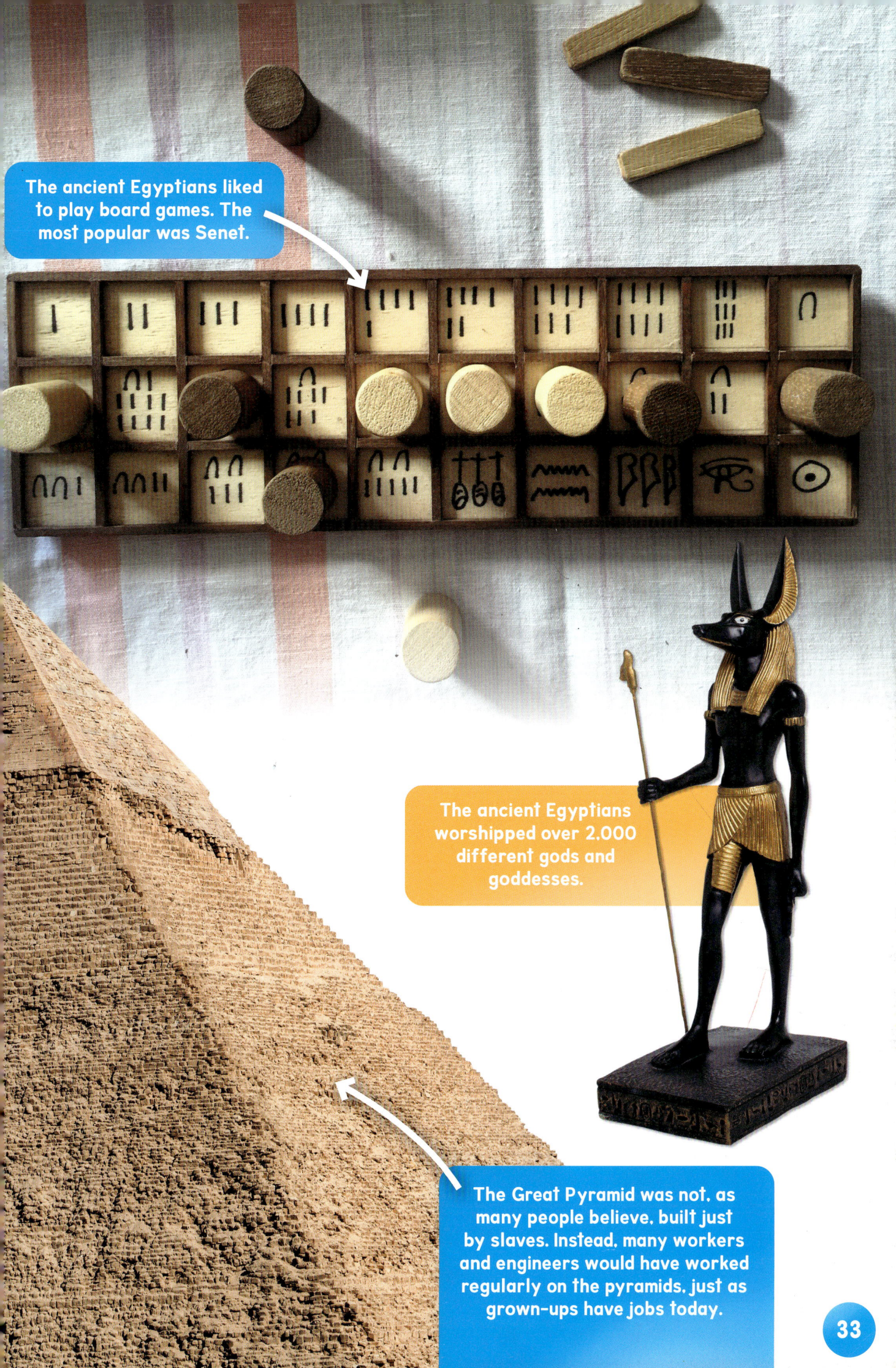

The ancient Egyptians liked to play board games. The most popular was Senet.

The ancient Egyptians worshipped over 2,000 different gods and goddesses.

The Great Pyramid was not, as many people believe, built just by slaves. Instead, many workers and engineers would have worked regularly on the pyramids, just as grown-ups have jobs today.

33

ACTIVITY

Can you complete this fun activity?

HOW TO MAKE YOUR OWN MUMMY HEAD

You will need:

A KNIFE

1 APPLE

Make sure you ask an adult for help!

80 GRAMS OF TABLE SALT

40 GRAMS OF BAKING SODA

A POT OR TUB BIG ENOUGH TO HOLD THE APPLE, WITH SOME EXTRA ROOM

MUMMIFICATION METHOD:

1. Ask your grown-up to help you cut a face out of the peel.

2. Place the apple into your tub. Pour in the baking soda and salt, enough to cover the apple completely.

3. After 14 days, take the apple out of the mixture. The mixture will have dried out the fruit, just like a mummy! The fruit did not rot because it was covered in the mixture.

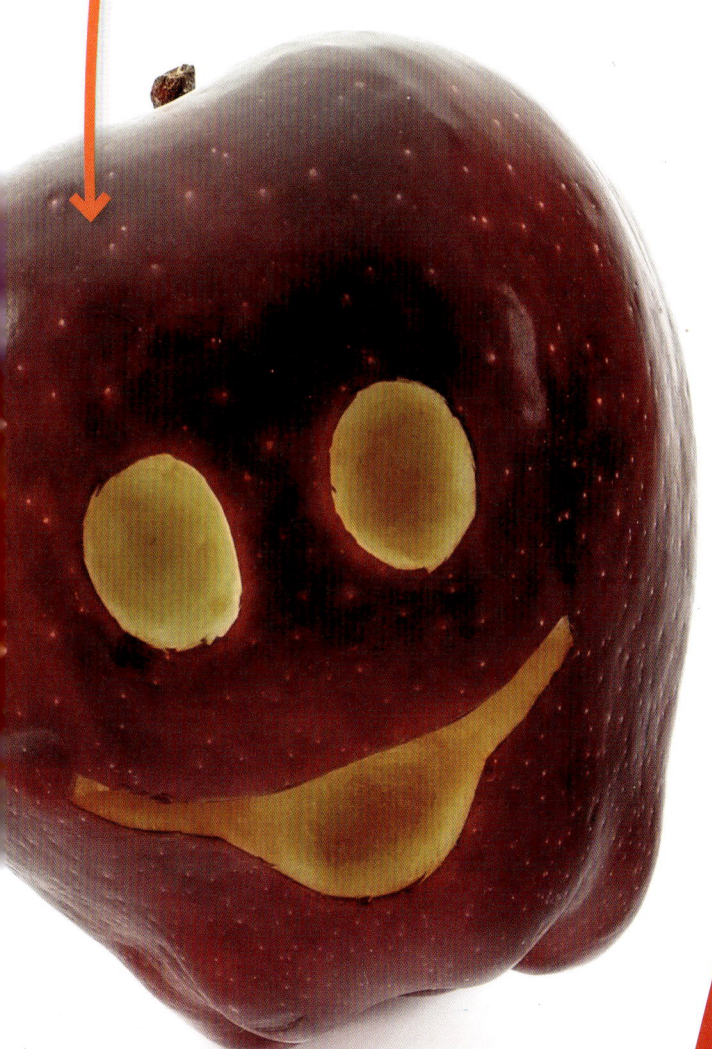

This is very similar to how mummies were made in ancient Egypt. They used a natural material called natron.

DO NOT eat your mummified head, or any of the ingredients!

QUICK QUIZZES

Can you beat these terrific tests?
3... 2... 1... GO!

MEMORY TEST

Can you answer these questions? Check back through the book if you're not sure.

1. **What were the kings and queens of ancient Egypt called?**

2. **Where were many of the early pharaohs buried?**

3. **What is the ancient Egyptian afterlife called?**

4. **What is this coffin-cover called?**

5. **What is ancient Egyptian picture-writing called?**

POP!
Pop quiz question! Who was at the very top of the social order, second only to the gods? Check page 22 for the answer!

Answers: 1. Pharaohs 2. In pyramids 3. The Field of Reeds 4. A sarcophagus 5. Hieroglyphs

GLOSSARY

A

afterlife the next part of life that comes after dying, which ancient Egyptians believed in

artefacts objects, such as tools or weapons, that were made by people in the past

B

bust a sculpture of a person's head and neck, sometimes also including a part of the shoulders and chest

C

conquers takes control of a country or city by force

crops plants that are grown by farmers for food or drinks

D

dairy made using milk

deity a god or goddess

E

engineers people who design and build complicated things, such as buildings and machines

H

harvest the gathering of plants ready to be made into food or drinks

I

internal organs parts of the body that have particular jobs, which can be found on the inside of the body

M

materials the things that objects are made of

P

peasants people who are poor, not educated and have low social status

poultry birds, such as chickens and ducks, that are raised on farms for their eggs or for meat

preserved kept in its original state or in good condition

R

rituals ordered actions that take place during religious ceremonies

S

sacred connected to gods or goddesses

sculpture a piece of art that is made by carving or moulding a material such as clay, stone and metal

slaves people who are owned by another person and are forced to work for that person without being paid

social order a system in which some people are more important than others

T

temple a building for worshipping gods and goddesses

tombs buildings or chambers above or below the ground that a dead body is kept in

toxic containing things that can be harmful

transport the ways of getting from one place to another

W

wealthy having a lot of money

INDEX

A

afterlife 12-13, 16, 18, 36

artefacts 7

C

canopic jars 17

crops 8-9, 12, 28

crowns 15

F

farmers 22, 31

Field of Reeds, the 16-17, 32

G

goddesses 4, 6, 12-13, 33, 37

gods 4, 6-7, 12-14, 16, 22, 26, 30, 32-33, 36-37

gold 4, 10, 15

government 6, 22

Great Sphinx, the 10, 20-21

H

hearts 16-17

hieroglyphs 4, 26-27

M

makeup 5, 24

mummies 4-5, 13, 17-18, 31, 34-35, 37

P

peasants 22

pharaohs 4, 10, 13-15, 18, 22-23, 30, 32, 36

pyramids 4, 10, 18-21, 30, 33

R

religions 6

River Nile, the 4, 8-9, 12, 28, 37

S

scribes 22, 26

servants 14, 22

slaves 14, 18, 22, 33

social orders 22, 36

T

teeth 25, 28

tombs 5, 18

V

vegetables 28